NO MORE HUSHING

THE TRUTH

NO MORE HUSHING THE TRUTH

Tiffany N. Wealth

Palmetto Publishing Group
Charleston, SC

No More Hushing the Truth
Copyright © 2020 by Tiffany N. Wealth
All rights reserved

First Edition

Printed in the United States

Paperback ISBN: 978-1-64990-020-3
eBook ISBN: 978-1-64990-021-0

CONTENTS

THE CLAN

Momma's child, Daddy's child, Momma and Daddy eloped. Daddy's old; Momma is old. History is gold, good gold, bad gold. Good soil and bad soil. The eight, from the eldest to the youngest, shackled by the impact of history. Far beyond what we can perceive. We all have eyes; we all have ears. We all have a body, spirit, and soul. The things we can't see will find a place to live. Smell, touch, taste, feel far beyond the natural. It all comes from somewhere; put a question mark there. Daddy's father, and his fathers, now let us remember Abraham's decedents. From the third and fourth generation. Lion of Judah, Prince of peace, he loves the tribe of eight. From the beginning to the end and to the beginning. Though we may wrestle, it is not against flesh and blood but the things above. There is an accuser of the brethren named Satan. Sabotage, generational curses, word curses, fear, death, torment, and turmoil. What a handful of tactics he brings. To steal kill and destroy. The named one knows our destiny; he knows what was birthed in us while in our mother's womb. When he reminds us of our past, we shall remind him of his future. Born into

sin but Christ had a plan. When we confess our sins, all things are washed away. Our future then becomes brighter than yesterday. An old seed can bring light if thrown on good ground. She rises; I rise. Rise, the tribe of eight. I am my sister's and brother's keeper sincerely the seventh.

HUSH

"Has anyone ever touched you?" Auntie asked me while sitting in the back seat. "Ahem." I hesitated while sitting next to Sissy. As I glanced at her, afraid, I stammered and said, "Somebody made me suck their big toe."

"Shush," Sissy said as she pinched my leg. "Hush," they said; Sissy obeyed their commands. Defenselessly, we were unable to speak. Lured and harassed, Church Boy intimidated us. "Hush, don't tell nobody." We both are scared, so we don't tell nobody, confused and abused. Who could have had a clue? "Shush, Sissy, don't speak." My face is hot; I can't speak. "Hush, don't tell anyone. We will be homeless if we give evidence." Now I can't speak. My mouth is shut; I can't breathe. "Shush, don't tell nobody. Surely one day you will testify."

THE OLD VERSUS THE NEW

Little girl x2, somebody stole your peace. Little girl x2—
oh, that's me. I heard you crying in your sleep. Little
girl x2, somebody stole your peace. Oh, little girl, yes,
that's me. I have a headache and no peace, no peace, x2
emotions running deep. Crying, "Ouch" in my sleep…lost
in the street and lost in me. Little girl x2 angry and
weak. That little girl doesn't even know me, and she
is playing hide-and-seek. Nine years old battered and
abused in the basement—they stripped me naked. Oh,
little girl, what's wrong with me? I encountered you
years ago; now it's time you leave. You give me no
peace, only mental fatigue. Little girl all grown up
now, the little caterpillar has found her crown. I did
not have a head covering; they stole my virginity and
braided my hair. With much prayer and fasting, I was
able to get free. I forgave them, because God forgave me.

PENNILESS

While homeless, going to and from on public
transportation, we frequently met others in
unfortunate situations. They panhandled and shook a
cup. *Can you spare some change*, they asked us?
Though we didn't have much, Momma still put some
change in their cups. She even bought food for some
with her government assistance card. I witnessed
Momma give when she didn't have much; she
showed compassion for those who struggled just like
us. Sometimes I cried, wishing I could sacrifice a
penny or two. I loathed to watch people sleep on the
street with little to no food to eat. Not all of them
struggled with addiction—surely Momma didn't.
Momma gave, interceded, and had faith. I admire
Momma for her courageous acts of sacrifice. In fact,
she hardly ever complained. She would sing us
hymns; "Saint John" was one and was my favorite melody.
I remember I clapped my hands off beat, in
a hooray. I asked Momma what that means. She gave
me a Duchenne smile and said to me, "God is the
author and finisher of the gospel; therefore, he is the
living word."

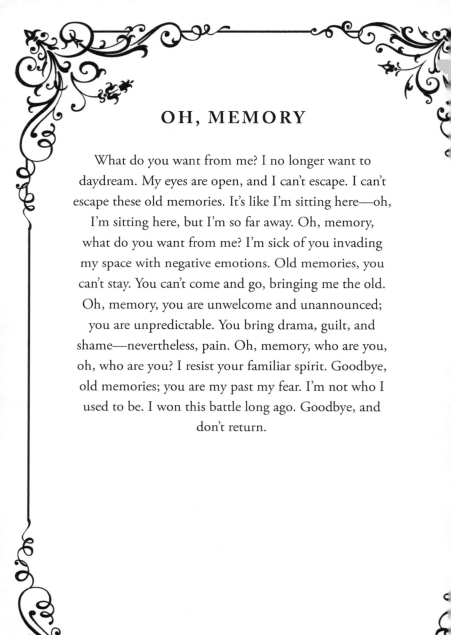

OH, MEMORY

What do you want from me? I no longer want to daydream. My eyes are open, and I can't escape. I can't escape these old memories. It's like I'm sitting here—oh, I'm sitting here, but I'm so far away. Oh, memory, what do you want from me? I'm sick of you invading my space with negative emotions. Old memories, you can't stay. You can't come and go, bringing me the old. Oh, memory, you are unwelcome and unannounced; you are unpredictable. You bring drama, guilt, and shame—nevertheless, pain. Oh, memory, who are you, oh, who are you? I resist your familiar spirit. Goodbye, old memories; you are my past my fear. I'm not who I used to be. I won this battle long ago. Goodbye, and don't return.

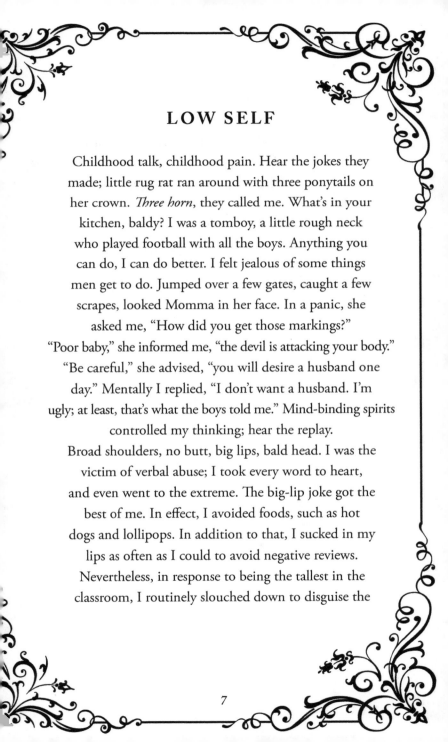

LOW SELF

Childhood talk, childhood pain. Hear the jokes they made; little rug rat ran around with three ponytails on her crown. *Three horn*, they called me. What's in your kitchen, baldy? I was a tomboy, a little rough neck who played football with all the boys. Anything you can do, I can do better. I felt jealous of some things men get to do. Jumped over a few gates, caught a few scrapes, looked Momma in her face. In a panic, she asked me, "How did you get those markings?" "Poor baby," she informed me, "the devil is attacking your body." "Be careful," she advised, "you will desire a husband one day." Mentally I replied, "I don't want a husband. I'm ugly; at least, that's what the boys told me." Mind-binding spirits controlled my thinking; hear the replay.

Broad shoulders, no butt, big lips, bald head. I was the victim of verbal abuse; I took every word to heart, and even went to the extreme. The big-lip joke got the best of me. In effect, I avoided foods, such as hot dogs and lollipops. In addition to that, I sucked in my lips as often as I could to avoid negative reviews. Nevertheless, in response to being the tallest in the classroom, I routinely slouched down to disguise the

broadness of my shoulders. It wasn't until the near
end of my adolescent years that I discerned that I
had become strongly impacted by every opinionated
imperfection regarding myself. In all honesty,
childhood talk, childhood pain, had the best of me.
Now look at me: my ashes have turned into beauty.

BARLETT BARNES

Youngest girl with seven siblings but felt alone, lived
in a home, started to feel like a ghost. If I had one
wish, get me out of the basement. In a dark pit, I was
undressed and forced against my will; those memories
never faded—better yet, they took part. Felt constant
pain, and other people's voice bombard my nut.
Lived in a world all alone. Momma and Daddy did not
know I lived with the big bad wolf. Some place we all
don't want to go. When I was nine, he stole my virginity;
later, he stole my identity. I lived with night terrors,
and I ruminated on the thought that I hate men.
Even in my sleep he attacked me; he would crawl into
my bed. Doctors called it sleep paralysis. All along I
knew I was the big bad wolf who would not leave me
alone. He whispered to me all my fears, enticed me
and placed me on a leash. Helpless and confused,
afraid to scream for help. I shouted loud as I could inside,
"Somebody get me out of here! Father God, if you can
hear me, please send Momma and Daddy an Amber
Alert. Help them to discern that this little girl isn't
home." No one knew where I was; neither did they
spot my support cane. Blind to reality, I lived in a
world so vain. All I knew was pain. As I fought for
my freedom, my head split; it felt as though it was an

earthquake. Lord God, please, no; leave my head alone. I pleaded for my sanity and hoped one day I would make it home.

TRIBULATIONS
OF THE EYES

I was taught to make eye contact when I speak. Gazing into other eyes made me fidget and have a fast heartbeat. I discovered a technique: I looked upon the bridge of people's noses while I spoke. Discomfort still arose, eye contact x2. I was told to make eye contact; believe me, it's an uncomfortable thing to do. It became difficult for me after childhood abuse. Lack of communication, low self-esteem, traumatic memories. Now it's polite to make eye contact! I had to muster up a lot of strength to fight for mental peace; making eye contact was far-fetched. It brought fear upon me. Fear of judgment, fear of disbelief, fear of vulnerability. When I looked into the eyes of those I trust, somehow, I was able to hold a gaze without worrying about things remaining discreet. It was those who I perceived misunderstood my wandering eyes. The shackling of my foot and the panic within me. Old sorrowful me…anxiety had the best of me. Eye contact x2. It was difficult for me to make eye contact. When I attempted to look into someone's eyes, discomfort would arise. My heart would beat at a fast rhythm, while a hunch of embarrassment invaded me. Abruptly, my gaze would shift into the sacred area of others as we spoke. My eyes had no regard; I often got angry with my wandering eyes. I avoided engaging in conversations because of my wandering eyes. I got tired of my wandering eyes, so I asked God to fix my wandering eyes.

STREETLIGHTS

I don't have anyone to look up to. Duck x2 goose,
I'm not making an excuse. Copycat, they called me,
cloned by my surroundings. "Bad news," he says. She
says, "What she says, I say." Faggot, watch your mouth
before you get a spanking. I isolate in my mind—don't
be fooled. I'm here next to you, but I'm out of space;
earth has my concentration. I replay everything I have
heard and seen…gosh, somebody erase these old
memories. I have learned all the wrong things—how I
should grade myself, well, honestly, I have low self-esteem.
I feel unworthy, I overthink everything, I fear
what happened to him may happen to me. I wish
what she had was mine—I swear, I will cheat and take
what she has and give her mine. Well that's all a
daydream. Now this is not a figurative speech; I want
what I see on TV. Make it my reality. Why can't what
they have be mine? Hmm, that's it…no more television.
Jealousy is a negative emotion; therefore, I need
someone to look up to and teach me more than just
how to tie my shoes. I have talent too; in an empty
piggy bank is where I stored it. I swear, if I don't
make it out of here, my dreams will become distorted.
Let me write this all down. I'm feeling like a hero now.
I found my role model; she's writing right now.

SUMMARY

I sat and brainstormed on Big Momma's couch. With suspicion, my thoughts had gone wild, clustered imaginations in a confused web. My emotions were altered and fickle all around. I pranced around in distress; I will not compromise despite my double mind. Hydra the mean beast has oppressed me. All day long he tempted me; had a blonde moment in Big Momma's seat. As I wrestled with the lies of the enemy, as a man thinketh, so is he. That's what the enemy said to me. Who said talk is cheap? Speak life, not defeat. Get you a covering; sit under a priest. Get out of Big Momma's seat; resist—do not agree with the lies of the enemy. Cast down his web, and put the beast back where be supposed to be. The Lord of Host has far greater power then Hercules, if you know what I mean. I leave you with this: use the word of God as your security. Surely the devil will flee, because he can't stand the heat.

I'M ONLY TWELVE

A marked bench…she sat on a bench called her bed,
with her head in between her legs. A mind full of
thoughts, she battled with herself and her alerted
eagle. "The devil is a lie," she declared as she pleaded
for help, attempting to quiet her mind. Those sticky,
stinky little thoughts would not leave the house of
Jarius. "Don't be afraid; just believe," Jesus declared.
Twelve-year-old Jarius rested on a marked bench
called her bed. Many gathered around as they wept in
sorrow; they professed, "Jarius is dead."
"She's not dead; she's asleep," he announced. The Master's words
calmed the commotion. Twelve-year-old Jarius
was troubled in her temple, troubled in the room of
her mind, body, and soul. There, she was tortured by
many ungodly spirits. Azrael entered an open window
of her homestead; her face was flushed, and she was
unresponsive. Those of her clan reported her as dead.
"Talitha Koum," Jesus spake.
At his very words, she rose and began to saunter
around. In the end, she ate and was a living miracle.

11307

Jane didn't cover me, poured my heart out to her on paper. While in juvey, I confessed to her that G&B molested me. I never received a reply; in the cell, I cried. Didn't understand how my pastor lacked compassion—at least that's how she made me feel. All I wanted was mercy, even the more I grieved. I didn't know what to think, due to a lack of understanding; I started to lose my mind. Thought about committing suicide. Fought just about every day; that became my new trade. I spoke with my hands, vowed to stand up for myself, since no one else demonstrated they could. I desperately wanted Jane to stand up for me; if I were her flesh and blood, surely she would. As a young child, I observed her speak her mind, so why not this time? I longed for her to defend me; why exactly didn't she write me? After months of no reply, I began to feel as though Jane didn't care if I died. In prison all alone—out of sight out of mind—I felt closer to my cellmates than those I knew on the outside. Told my social worker I didn't want to go back home, begged for him to place me in a new home. I did not want to live in a dysfunctional home. My peers viewed me as strong, because I bullied them all around as I played the lesbian role. Maybe if I still had my innocence, I would be a bit sweet. Only the Father knew the truth behind my antics, so I went ahead and prayed. Listen to the dialogue: Father God, please help me. I'm not a bad person; I pretend to be. I figured if I hid behind a shale, that would keep me protected. Lord, you know what I mean.

SWIPER, NO SWIPING

Farted and sneezed, yeah, the little church girl sprays.
Raised my tail and hissed, used my best judgment
as my weapon of defense while practicing my
offense. Predator, take this; I carried around a scent.
Stomped on the devil's head, wood pussy won't miss.
Hissed a little word or two, stamped my feet and
raised my tail. Go away. I resist. Digest this. I'm saved,
hum to that, go pray. Won't trap me in a cage; I saw
your sheet from far away. I can see my target, for
Christ's sake—the breath of life resides in all creation.
Christ communicated with the ravens. "Very good,"
Christ said as he looked at all he made.

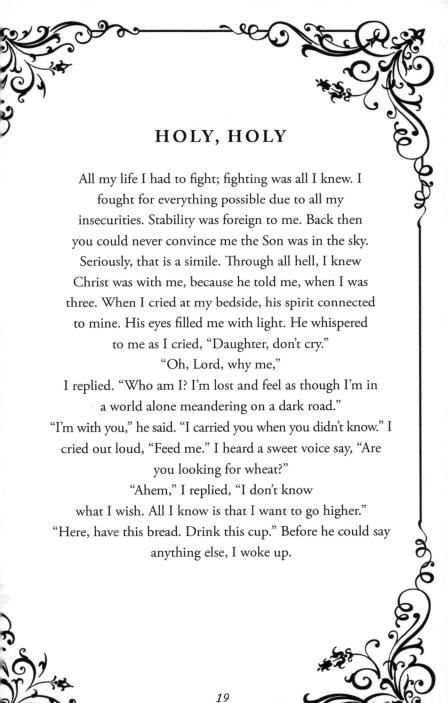

HOLY, HOLY

All my life I had to fight; fighting was all I knew. I
fought for everything possible due to all my
insecurities. Stability was foreign to me. Back then
you could never convince me the Son was in the sky.
Seriously, that is a simile. Through all hell, I knew
Christ was with me, because he told me, when I was
three. When I cried at my bedside, his spirit connected
to mine. His eyes filled me with light. He whispered
to me as I cried, "Daughter, don't cry."
"Oh, Lord, why me,"
I replied. "Who am I? I'm lost and feel as though I'm in
a world alone meandering on a dark road."
"I'm with you," he said. "I carried you when you didn't know." I
cried out loud, "Feed me." I heard a sweet voice say, "Are
you looking for wheat?"
"Ahem," I replied, "I don't know
what I wish. All I know is that I want to go higher."
"Here, have this bread. Drink this cup." Before he could say
anything else, I woke up.

WARRIOR AT HAND

A demon shut her mouth; she was afraid to speak.
Did not realize she could not because a demon shut
her up. She cried her eyes out. Threw temper
tantrums. Growled like a dog and clenched her fist
because she could not get her words out. She hated
everyone, especially Momma and Daddy; in her
thoughts she spoke loudly: "Why is no one is helping
me?" She felt helpless and cried herself to sleep. She
muttered a prayer and said, "Father God, please help
me; I am becoming truly angry." That moment he gave
her a pen; that very moment he became her best
friend. She wrote on the page of her notebook: *Will I
ever speak again?* As she wrote tears rolled down her
face because she felt his very presence. As she held
her notebook firmly, with a nurturing monotone, he
asked her, "Who told you that you would die?"
"Nobody, God, I just feel I'm suffocating inside. Please don't let
me die." She was afraid to close her eyes. "Rest," he said.
She had puffy eyes and a headache from crying
because she was free to speak and say the things she
had wanted to say all along. As she fought her sleep,
she begged Daddy not to leave her alone. She felt a
sweet breeze as she dozed off to sleep. When

morning came, she realized all she had jotted down had been washed away. Christ removed the muzzle Satan had placed. She discovered that Christ had given her back her speech. With that very pen, she spoke again because the demon was driven out.

BABBLE

I have said dreadful things, cut individuals with my
tongue, all because I feared the opinion of them.
Engaged in a few scuffs because I would not shut up.
I don't say this to rhyme, but if I could go back into
time, I'll renege my very own words. I pray for those I
hurt; forgive me. I didn't know the power of words.
Now I discern that words can curse. Life and death
lie in the power of the tongue. Christ made creation
with his very own speech. Everything he spoke
manifested. Be wise in your speech, for you will reap
what you sow. Frightfully, if I can go back in time, I'll
tell my old self. The fear of man will crush you; don't
convert to your audience dynamic. I will say this to
her face because her conduct was not in step with the
truth of the gospel. Pause before you speak. Don't use
harsh speech. Obey the living word; know that
whatever is in you comes out of you. Avoid
misconduct and R-rated idioms. Keep it PG-13. Amen,
touch and agree.

CHORUS TO HEAVEN

Give me a pure heart; wash me clean. Sprinkle me
with hyssop, and make me white as snow. Purge me
from all impurity. Give me a new spirit. Wake me up
again so that my heart may feel secure. Don't leave
me alone. As I write in tears of sorrow, keep a record
on your scroll. And I will play a harp and a lyre to you
before the sun rises. Selah.

BOAT TALK

Holy how high, never seen the righteous forsaken.
Young, olde nor his seed begging bread. Do you love
me? I repeat, do you love me? Again, do you
absolutely love me times three? Sorry to hurt you; I
don't mean to antagonize you. Just have a little riddle
for you. Do you love me more than this, or that? Baa,
feed my sheep. You herd that? Surely one day you
will grow old; when you were young, you dressed
yourself. You integrated with your flock. But when
you are mature, you will look up, and someone else
will clothe you and escort you where you reject to go.
Grasp all of what I spoke. Therefore, you will know
who he is because he called them friends. And did
many things.

HOOD INTERCESSION

I'm from the hood. I lived in the hood, fought in the hood. Now the altar is where I fight. The pew is where I live; the oil is what I rep. Put your set up, yeah, it's a setup, cross up. I represent the King. I won't renege; I've been baptized by the oath of his blood. What an honor to give dap to tambourines. I'm recruiting sheep; say a little prayer with me. Confess and believe unashamedly that Christ is king. Powwow in prayer under the star of Israel. Be brave and take a knee like John Doe. Hold your head up, smile for real. Stand your ground, and don't be moved, like the Statue of Liberty. Wear your armor and remember, I'm not your rival—I'm his secretary. I'm going to the pin to remind him of his promises. I will keep no peace, neither day nor night in mention of his name, until he answers our prayers. Indeed sincerely, brothers and sisters of the struggle, strap up with the palms of your hands and pray for our communities. Oh, what a melody that will be to bring peace and unity.

EXHORTATION

Hasbian, let me tell you where I been. I was once a
lesbian, wore snap backs and jogging pants. Played
the role of a man, confused in my identity, wrestled
against his plan. Affected by low self-esteem, dared
not to be the weaker vessel. Hid behind my clothing,
was angry with my younger self. *Hush*—that's what
they told me. Who told you silence is gold? I hate to
disagree, paid into defeat. Traumatic memories
muzzled me. Shut me up like the mouth of a lion.
Contrary bit deep, a violent roar of misery. Abuse,
neglect, a bloody heart misery—fear, hate, rage, all the
above. Lost with issues purging blood. In a world all
alone, I wondered was I alone. In the mirror tears
rolled, tied a rope around my neck. Walked me to a
cage. There I went, caged in self-hate, had my head
behind a gate. A story told I once heard held onto
vicarious hurt. Gave me constant turmoil and
nightmares, didn't understand what I heard, or even
observed. Too young to understand, a little spy that I
was vivid—images in my nut. Came through my young
ears, a family's secrets reviled. John Doe molested the
eldest, a gasp of unbelief. No, not the preacher man

who sings! A question of am I next? I well-rehearsed. *Jesus, please protect me.* As I prayed, I grunted my teeth. Fear knew my name; callousness stiffened my heart. Fell into a deep sleep—that's where I found peace. At nine years old, I was abused, molested by perverse teens who belonged to the ministry. A double dose of pure hate. While in pain, I prayed. Didn't know what to think or feel, just wanted to know what I did. Made a promise to myself: When I grow big and strong, I will go after them. If I were a judge, I would give them life in prison, bang a gavel, and put them in cuffs. All the hate I felt toward them…it wasn't until I wrote it on a dotted line and signed. Lord, heal me! In due time he sprinkled me with hyssop. I guess there is power in the pen. Read that again.

HEAVEN SEES ME

"I don't have time," I said, as I looked into the spiritual
mirror of my eyes. Christ sketched out a beautiful
design. The enemy tried to destroy the work of his
hands. But Christ blew the ashes. Beauty am I, or am I
not. "I do not have time," I said. This very hour I'll
rearrange the analog. Lay my hands on the mirror
and scream. It's time for some dialogue. Pick up the
phone; Christ has called. Christ, talk to me, tell me
who I am since the fall. Ahh. It's easy to blame Adam
and Eve, but Lord, I ask that you have mercy on them.
The accuser of the brethren is Satan; he's full of lies
and schemes. So, Daddy, enlighten me; you said you
would never to me. The mirror is fogging—I can
barely see. I pointed my finger at the mirror; one
pointed back at me. Using the foggy mirror, he wrote
a passage to me. His message was, *You're beautiful and
sweet. I made every part of you and called it good.*
Lord, tell me the truth! I do not want to lie in the
mirror. He sketched a design onto the mirror. I
stared at his creation with my muddy eyes. He said to
me, *Pay attention; that is you.* I exhaled and
stammered over my speech. I then said, "Please

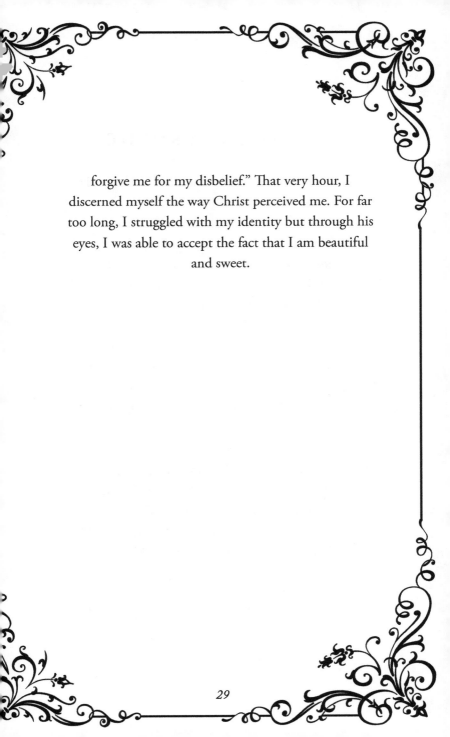

forgive me for my disbelief." That very hour, I
discerned myself the way Christ perceived me. For far
too long, I struggled with my identity but through his
eyes, I was able to accept the fact that I am beautiful
and sweet.

THE BOXING PROPHET

Vowed to get in the ring, wanted to be the people's champ, you know what I mean. I'll fight for my dreams; I had a little fight in me. Internal pain motivated me, trained hard as I could six days a week. I refused to be beat, banged on the heavy bag, thought about all my pain. Channeled my anger as I trained, increased confidence I gained. Dedicated myself in the gym like it was my sanctuary. As I refrained from the streets, I changed my old ways, and learned not to gang bang. GD was what I claimed—my first bout I had my hand raised as the golden gloves champion. "Yo, that girl is extraordinary; surely, she shall be world champion one day," I overheard spectators say. More inspiration I gained, bobbed and weaved as I trained, wanted to get my family out of poverty. Hmm, who could roger that, you must be quicker than that, hand and feet coordination were exceptional. You could bet a buck. I patted myself on the back, self-talked as I trained; my imagination was my greatest tool. My self-discipline and determination are why others gave accolades and praise due to my hard work and dedication. Had a team of family not friends; it was in my nature to represent. Told my trainers my desire to be the people's champ. Prophesied over my dreams, used my talents for Christ's sake, knowing that one day he will surely make room. I shall keep my hand raised as I follow him.

WORLDLY CHURCH BACKSLIDERS

There is no sanctification in this house; this house is cluttered…I saw a mouse. I hear a lot of squeaky noise, lay members affected by hasty speech. Ouch, don't scratch me. I was attacked near the seats of my neighbor's glass house. Peekaboo, I see through you. Church mice, I saw a few, more than a dozen. Refused to practice what they preached; forgot their very own sermon while walking back to their seats. They stood around watching, the evil eye, is what they gave me. They clicked up and claimed their seats. Please do not seat here; this area is reserved for the elite. Though I was not appointed, that didn't stop anyone from being intimidated by my anointing. Oh, Lord, too much drama in the ministry. Gifted but few are chosen; all love the Lord, but very few demonstrate the fruits of his laboring. More than a dozen refuse to practice what they preach. Forget their very own sermon as they walk back to their seats. Learned behavior, muscle memory, the apple doesn't fall too far from the tree. Leave me alone, Eve; the King said not to eat from that tree. Lord, help me protect my

garments. They ushered me in, then forced me out,
didn't want me to be a gift to the house. Witnessed
tug-of-war brawls through competition, what really had
their attention. Lost sight of the cross; I had seen a lot of
lost blood. The terrors attacked the weak sheep while
predators preached suggestive sermons. Who did they
think they had fooled? I spotted their dirty moves.
Because spiritually they wore mismatched shoes.
False prophets wanted me to give up my seat; I
refused to leave until the Lord released me. He
brought me there to clean house and drive out
demonic vows.

SILENT NIGHT

Stop cliquing up and talking with your black boots. I
object your dirty moves. Learn a new language; too
much talking will make you sin. Get a pen and write
by his hand; love has good italics. Roger that, here, sign
with that. Throw no shade; remove your horseshoes.
And hush your heavy lips. Beware—your topic is
subject to cause and effect, because your mask is
plastic. By the spirit I know you. I'm not the one to
judge you. I can't be a slave to sin under the care of a
madman. I must point you in the right direction: "Go
north," Parks said. Now pick up your bed and walk
toward the light of salvation. Stop shacking up in a
glass house. He gave you five chances; come from
among them now.

RIDICULED BUT CHANGED

Have you ever served a past sentence? Have you ever been in bondage or oppressed and labeled as a mess— better yet, no good? Have you ever walked past a mirror and seen a black sheep with tears in her eyes?

Black sheep, lesbian, fornication, baa. I herd that ridicule. Baa…Jesus delivers; I thought you knew. Herd, my petition against ridicule, flock up and shut up—be a good shepherd. Point no more fingers at me. I'm new; speak no more negativity. Shush, silence, hush up with your black boots. That's a dirty move. About face, now salute. I'm on the right track hungry for pasture God food. Throw no more stones at this house, for he lives in me. Rather, you believe it or not. Stop holding on to my past like an Easter egg basket, you filthy rabbit. Cracking old eggs, snaggletooth. I have been ridiculed; I have been forgiven. I am new— believe it or not, I owe no explanation. His name is engraved in my forehead, lion of Judah. Exclamation point! Exactly. He did it for me; he will do it for you. No more ridicule, baa, baa, black boots. You have been petitioned; it's already been written.

SEVEN TIMES

Lord, forgive me for my sins, and help others realize
no sin is greater than another. For we all fall short of
your glory. As I walked into the sanctuary, all eyes
were on me. I took a seat people; scooted away from
me, looked at me like I had leprosy. Turned up their
noses at me, unclean x2. "Unclean," the preacher said. "Sin
stinks." I was doomed with embarrassment, wanted to
retaliate in his very presence. Little did they know, my
heart ached with pain. I was full of shame and
desperately wanted to change. Didn't know what to
do or say. With a heart of repentance, I proclaimed, "I
know I'm in sin; please lay your hands." Follow my
advice, for I saddle my donkey and head out to my
house. Second Samuel seventeen and twenty-three.
Rest in peace, Ahithophel.

OWL

Peace be still to the civilians. Where are the Samaritans? They all walked out of class troubled by violence. The good going bad buckling up, bargaining cash. Better check the receipt; they are stocking up. That's called preparation. They're exchanging bonds preparing for the future, don't want to be left behind. Breathe in, breathe out—better carry an oxygen tank around. I see people expiring like expiration dates, getting caps popped in them like canned goods. No one is safe; they're on every side of the scope. Violence is crowding me. I'm in panic mode. I hated to see a loved one on a tombstone. Rest in peace. I see a lot of graffiti. Send me a halo; I prayed for an angel. Hallowed be thou name, Father God, I pray; give me the strength I need to stay on the right side of the street. Sincerely, yours truly.

BLUE LINE CORRUPTION

The first day I made an impression; then came interrogation. Millions of questions from more than one race. I was the victim of separation and hate; it is true—misery does love company. Hear the questions they asked me. "Why do you want to be a police officer?"

"Why do you ask?" I replied. "Is it because I'm female?" Sexism and racism, I experienced the first week. I know it's rare for women to want to be police; at least that's what some men think. I chuckled. A fool must have raised you; that's not how gentlemen think. Show some chivalry, respect my badge, welcome me with respect. I wore my badge, bold and proud; disbelief filled their eyes. That very moment I got bullied on the job. No matter my work ethic, I was still rejected. They threw my reports around and laughed at me out loud. Told false testimonies to the chief, with intent to damage my reputation. Behaved like teenage kids, spread phony rumors about me without a telephone ring. Turned the entire department against me. In roll call they segregated me, would not let me take a seat. They failed to discern it was God who hired me. I was an

officer among wolves, and I was the only sheep. Of
course, they felt threatened by me; they did not
understand how I can be wise as a snake and
harmless as a dove and refuse to be corrupt. Again,
"Why do you want to be a police officer!" They dared to
know. Oh, my, they asked me, forced me to give a
response. Gosh, did I mention they said they would
get me drunk? "Hang around a little longer; sooner or
later you won't be sober." When they realized they
couldn't win me over, they were convinced that I was
undercover. Created new rules because of me, bossed
me around. Sergeants were arrogant and proud.
Commanded me to adhere to their rules or else I
would be written up for—what's that word?—
insubordination. Blamed everything on the rookie,
had no one to vouch for me. They deceived the chief
and turned him against me. Terminated me with little
to no evidence; I was the victim of hearsay. Your
magistrate, may I speak sincerely? Either hired or fired,
I will remain an officer, because I belong to the king;
ask David, he will tell you. Sorry, Saul, I intimidated
you all. I thought I took an oath just like y'all.

THEY HATE MY BELLY

Let me give you a shovel; I want the truth. They tried
to bury me with lies and plotted on another lie. Wow,
what a habitual lie, pee-yew, achoo, allergic to fools
who hate to tell the truth. Lies, all these lies, told my
father a lie, but he knows the truth. Their fate was to
bury me, wanted to put me in the grave before time.
Get off my soil with them black boots; hand me that
shovel while I dust off this coat of mine. Yeah, I
know you despise colorful things; can't understand
why he gave it to me. I had a dream that one day I
would stand in the face of my enemies. I had a dream
that one day I would deliver thee oppressed. Dreamer,
what a dream. I'm a kingpin, belly so fat like an
orphanage kid. I guess that's why they tried to bury
me and sell me, wanted to sabotage the fulfillment of
my dream. What a miracle to be called by my name
and rise again. Indeed, Christ is my friend; he
unraveled me in the face of those who said I was
dead. All Christ did was call my name. Then, I stood in
place.

WISE COUNSEL

Know those who labor among you. Believe the things revealed to you. Pay attention to actions, not speech. Keep your dear friends close to you. Beware that an enemy can be right under your nose. They camouflage themselves in sheep's clothing, per se perpetrate themselves. I suppose you know what I mean. Don't be naive; beware of Judas schemes. Even Jesus was handed over to the authorities. Knock, knock, did that ring a bell? Everyone who comes across your path is not sent to help; some are sent to bring crucifixion. Ask one of the twelve—Judas didn't help; he betrayed his Master.

AMEN

It was good for me to suffer. I suffered and went down the wrong path. Lord, you're good, and what you do is good. I take delight in your law. It is worth more than silver and gold. You created me with your very own hands. Help me to understand your commands. I'm a friend to those who have respect for you. I praise you and refuse to socialize with fools. You were faithful to your promise when you made me suffer. All of my past troubles were for a greater purpose. As I moan and groan on this writing paper, in the heavens you watch from above. Your omnipresence comforts me. I noted that from the book of Isaiah fifty-seven and fifteen. You received the heart of the contrite. Never left me, neither did you forsake me. That is why I am a believer of your word. I understand that everything has its limits. The day I meandered in the wilderness, there you found me. In the past I was oblivious of my sins; in the hot sun I crawled on my knees and lay under a fig tree. I rehearsed the salvation prayer, doubted my very own words. Didn't know you were in the garden. Hid myself with fig leaves, saw a negative reflection of myself. Oh, Lord, have mercy on me. For far too long, I have been deceived.

DESPERATE BEE

I'm so favored; you'll swear I'm clever. I have no
Tricks, I'm just desperate. A servant, not a worker. Seek
and you shall find. Daddy, can I have some milk and
honey? Ask and you shall receive. Ouch, I just got a bee
sting. Honey Christ bestowed unto me. In awe, I
spoke in unknown tongues as my tongue panted in
hallelujah chords. I had an epiphany and began to see
the mysterious. Anoint your head with oil; ask and you
shall receive a remarkable blessing. Ever seen a
queen evangelize and sing? Cheers, this bee has
honey. It's an altar call—want some milk and honey? With
wise lips I bless you with a holy kiss. You have been
renewed. What a benediction! Farewell, my friend.

ABOUT THE AUTHOR

Tiffany Wealth has experienced a lot of tragedy in her life, much of it stemming from her adolescence and early adult years. Throughout her life, she has especially struggled with her identity. In spite all she faced, she never gave up on her faith. Thanks to her resilience and determination, she was able to make positive strides toward a better future.

Starting at a young age, writing was Tiffany's number one way to communicate with the world. She would write prayers, poems, and short stories to help work through her many internal battles. In her writing she found healing, and she gained a remarkable relationship with God. Tiffany now uses writing to encourage and provoke others never to give up, and to realize that no matter how bad things seem, healing and deliverance are always possible.